INSPIRED FROM Beyond

THE ESSENCE OF A PAST LOVE

Co-created by

MONICA REDFORD AND DAVE

Copyright © 2024 Monica Redford and Dave.

All rights reserved. No part of this book may be reproduced, stored, or transmitted by any means—whether auditory, graphic, mechanical, or electronic—without written permission of both publisher and author, except in the case of brief excerpts used in critical articles and reviews. Unauthorized reproduction of any part of this work is illegal and is punishable by law.

ISBN: 978-1-63950-262-2 (sc)
ISBN: 978-1-63950-263-9 (e)

This publication contains the opinions and ideas of its author. It is intended to provide helpful and informative material on the subjects addressed in the publication. The author and publisher specifically disclaim all responsibility for any liability, loss, or risk, personal or otherwise, which is incurred as a consequence, directly or indirectly, of the use and application of any of the contents of this book.

Writers Apex

Gateway Towards Success

8063 MADISON AVE #1252
Indianapolis, IN 46227
+13176596889
www.writersapex.com

INTRODUCTION

This is a true story of a young romance and a metaphysical experience of connection after death. It shares love and happiness and the sorrow of never finding a way back together. The concept of love as being valid *until death do us part and in sickness and in health* does not necessarily have to be the only experience one can have. In matters of the heart, there is never any time limit on what love a heart can hold. Apparently, I had to learn a lesson that love is, and always will be, what really matters in a lifetime and in the afterlife. The experiences and people we meet cannot be taken for granted, as each of us is a teacher regardless of whether the experience is painful or joyful during our soul's journey.

DEDICATION

I dedicate this book to Michele Love, Intuitive Medium, RMT and Vibrational Astrologer at Healing Inspirations, a holistic healing and learning center in Liverpool, New York. If her understanding of Twin Flames was not available, I never would have understood the dark, painful years ahead. I also never would have known in which direction to look when I was searching for answers.

To my children, Dava, Michael, and Gina, who never criticized the journey I led during their growing-up years and, instead, supported me with love and respect, truly the best gift a mother can receive.

"They are not dead who live in the hearts they leave behind."
~ Tuscarora

This saying was taken from a Native book of Wisdom. There is no specific author, other than the nation listed.

CHAPTER 1

There are so many quotes and inspirations to help us move on when we enter a space in time that we did not plan. People will encourage you with generic quotes or persuade you to move on when you encounter crises, sickness, personal setbacks, or death, but sometimes you just have to go through the process of pain to understand the lesson. This is my story to share—an afterlife experience with a past love. I have said to the many skeptics, "Just because you haven't experienced it, doesn't mean it can't exist." The experience of grieving for someone after 50 years of not being in a relationship with that person was never dreamed of in my life's game plan. I have carried my story primarily alone, which made this journey so much harder to bear. Even so, it can never take away the experiences of genuine love I have had with others, nor will I close the door to ever love again.

I love the quote by Brené Brown, "When we deny our stories, they define us. When we tell our own stories we get to write the ending." I own this story, as painful as it is, and my attempt to convey it. I was never aware anything like this could happen. The most traumatizing experience was the inability to share my daily struggles with others as I searched for a way to relieve my grief. When I tried to express my frustrations to others, I would always know if my story was not being received, despite the person's kindness and politeness. Due to my emotional suffering, I began to write to release the confusion and pain I felt. If I use the word love when writing to this beloved, it is because I cannot find an appropriate word to convey my feelings. It has taken nearly four years for this short story to bring some understanding to print. And so my story begins.

CHAPTER 2

After a second divorce, I kept myself busy with buying and restoring a few homes, and then moved on to developing a small baking business as I worked my full-time job as a secretary. These roles could not erase the solitude I felt—or the frustration and loneliness at times. I questioned my attractiveness and the reasons for the failure of my marriages. During that time, I truly wanted a person in my life, but the idea of using the internet for dating was not right for me. When I did try the internet for a few months, it confirmed what I believed—that this means of meeting someone would not help me sense the chemistry I needed in selecting a person. I continued to keep busy with the hope someone would just walk into my life.

Years passed, marked with my children's weddings, grandchildren being born and the many house moves due to being unsettled within myself. Few real vacations to relax and enjoy were ever taken. I looked forward to family visits with children, who lived at a distance. During those years, with everyday work as a secretary and home maker, I found an interest in metaphysical philosophies and became an Usui and Karuna Reiki Master. I didn't realize I would face much uncertainty with a forced retirement or how much spirituality and holistic healing would be needed to help me move on. I practiced Reiki as a volunteer at a local hospital, work which may have helped me more than the patients. I also did a lot of work on myself to heal and took my soul's journey seriously. The anger over the unexpected, forced retirement with no financial back-up plan caused incredible confusion and loss, monetarily and emotionally. Then, having my elderly father living with me was another factor taking my energy and quickly eating up the years now passing me by.

CHAPTER

In the summer of 2014, I attended a class on Twin Flames taught by Michele Love, medium and vibrational astrologist working at Healing Inspirations, a holistic healing center and shop located near Syracuse, New York. I didn't find it necessary to worry about or seek my Twin Flame (also known as Twin Soul) but chose to do one of her suggestions anyway. She asked the class to write a letter to their Twin Flame angel. Everyone has an angel and, yes, I always believed that, and I skeptically questioned why this was necessary. I wrote a note to this newly named angel, tossed it in a drawer and forgot about it until much later. The note said: "Dear Angel of Twin Flame, I need someone to share my life who has the same values, goals, interests, and, especially, who fits in with my family. Please, before the end of the year, send someone who is waiting for me."

By the end of November, I received the sad news that Dave, an ex-boyfriend who I dated almost 50 years ago, had passed. It shook me to the core yet I couldn't anticipate the raw emotions that would follow. While rearranging a drawer, I rediscovered my angel letter before the end of the year. Without even considering that his death may have been an answer to the angel request, I wept uncontrollably without knowing why. When I reflect on my reaction to hearing of his death and my experience at the wake and funeral, my emotions seem extreme for someone who had not been in a relationship with Dave for decades. This was before I started writing and spending so much time and money to learn how and why something like this could happen.

CHAPTER

4

An explanation of Twin Flames or Twin Souls (not to be confused with soul mates) is where one soul splits into two before they come to earth. One soul gravitates more toward spiritual existence and the other toward material existence. I did not completely buy this theory. I never heard of it before the class, but apparently there are many people who have experienced this and are compelled to write or speak about it. As people are becoming enlightened in their spirituality, they are waking up to understandings that—although they were not taught these perspectives earlier—have been around since the beginning of time. These enlightened people are usually sensitive and will pick up on things other people take for granted. A lesson on Twin Flame (www.TwinFlame.com) reads:

Being on the Twin Flame journey does not mean you need to be in a relationship with someone, it merely requires you to be in a relationship with yourself, to become strong, devotional and on purpose; to seek out your short comings and rise above all shadow and darker aspects of your soul so that a harmonization occurs. We become balanced and whole in ourselves and each other. Why can't they find each other? There is some disconnectedness, some veil that keeps them separated yet they are so close.

Though we may not understand why we have separated, there is a reason that is higher than ourselves that is helping us to learn lessons on earth such as detachment, forgiveness, surrender, inner strength, and trust. Twin Flame is not a pleasant ordeal and will leave one with a string of questions in your head with no real answers. The interesting part is you never feel disconnected.

Gary Zukav explains in his book, *Soul to Soul: Communications from the Heart*, "(R)elationships illuminate the parts of our personalities that are unhealed—such as the parts that dominate others, please others, judge others, and exploit them. As long as you haven't addressed those tendencies in yourself, you will attract problematic relationships into your life and recreate these issues until they're healed. However, once you heal a part of your personality, the playing field changes. You no longer need an abusive relationship, or a dependent one. You no longer need to dominate someone, be submissive to another, or be jealous and possessive. When that part of your journey is complete, it frees you to create true intimacy with a different kind of partner."

Elizabeth Gilbert writes, "People think a soul mate is your perfect fit and that's what everyone wants. But a true soul mate is a mirror, the person who shows you everything that is holding you back, the person who brings you to your own attention so you can change your life."

Most metaphysical experts who've I met with this understanding feel my experience is Twin Flame. I really don't care how one defines it, but—based on the research I have done—I most definitely have experienced the separation, pain, and grief that fits the description of when one soul departs.

CHAPTER

Sitting at a restaurant, a week before Thanksgiving 2014, a former classmate informed me of Dave's passing. My feelings were of shock and then sadness. I questioned people, but no one knew what had happened. I knew I would learn more at his wake.

It wasn't until the wake, I learned of his health issues. He went to the doctor's office one November day and had a heart attack. He was admitted to the hospital and died. The family told me there was nothing the doctors could do to save him. As I approached the casket, I struggled to view him; a man who looked nothing like the man I remembered. Dave had been a caregiver who chose to sacrifice his own well-being for others. He was often warned that he was gambling with his own life. He was encouraged to get the open-heart surgery that his body was visibly telling him was needed. I learned later he was putting his partner first and didn't know how he could balance recovery from an operation for himself and with caregiving. Over the years, I was not aware this man was not taking good care of his own life. Although I used to think that eventually I would bump into him somewhere in town, I never felt the urgency to force it.

I met his adult children in the receiving line at the wake for the first time. I was asked by his daughter and son how I knew their father. I said, "I went to school with him." They asked my name and, when I told them, they immediately replied, "Our Dad spoke of you." I was flattered yet surprised, wondering when he would have spoken of me. Joking, I asked if they heard the story about the driving lesson. They laughed and said, "Yes, he told us."

The driving lesson experience: Over the years, regardless of what stage of my life I was in, I had the odd experience of bursting into laughter whenever the memory crossed my mind of an evening when Dave and I were on a double date with my sister, Kathy, and her husband, Mike. The memory of one particular night always stuck with me. Dave had a new red convertible and he allowed me to drive it that night. I took the wheel with no fear. As we were rounding a corner, I let the steering wheel slip through my fingers and the car ended up sideways on a sloped hill. The car was at a tilt with the potential to roll. When I turned around, Kathy and Mike were thrown to one side of the car unable to get out due to the angle we were in. Dave jumped into action and somehow managed to get us out of the car with the help of Mike and someone who heard the racket and came running to assist in moving the car safely off the hill.

Dave asked, "What were you thinking while steering the car?" I replied, "I thought I saw on TV you can let the wheel spin through your fingers and for some reason instead of gripping the wheel tightly I let it slide through my fingers." It was the only time I ever saw Dave unamused. It made the memory ten times more enjoyable.

In my reflecting on this, it was my private moment of a sick sense of humor, and it always made me smile. He was patient and kind to me always, but I don't recall ever getting a driving lesson again. Now, since his passing, I have never been as amused by this as I had been over the decades.

CHAPTER

When I watched the series of pictures of Dave's life at the funeral home, I was taken aback. All of a sudden, I thought to myself, "How did I forget the essence of him?" I understood there would be some nostalgia, but this was different, and I questioned, "Why am I feeling this way?"

Speaking to one of his sisters, she said his body could not withstand the heart attack and possibly, even if he had lived, he might not have been the same. She questioned where he would have been able to live if he had recovered. I did all I could to stop myself from saying, "But I would have taken him in." This was the second time in my memory I questioned something about us out of the blue that did not logically make sense to ask. I was more caught up with questioning why I felt this desire to help when nothing had happened between us for so many years. It was just an inner awareness. I also didn't question why she made such a comment. Why wouldn't he have gone back to the woman with whom he was living?

The following day, I went to the funeral. The priest spoke of Dave's many acts of kindness throughout his life. At communion, I walked by the casket and touched it as my last goodbye. In the final moments of the mass, the tears flooded down my cheeks. I left quickly. Without understanding why, I would continue to cry for many days. Then, days turned into months and then years. I was shocked that I was so overwhelmed and could not process what was happening.

To find some peace, I was inspired to write a post as a tribute on a Facebook prayer circle referring to my thoughts after the wake. I wrote:

> "I know these words may be confusing, but I am just expressing loss. Tonight I visited the wake of a beloved from years ago. It was one of those moments when you wondered what if I should have seen him one more time, the memories, his wonderful family and a slew of thoughts that made you realize he was a small part of what became part of me. I realized as I said words to him tonight, the prayer for his family and the knowledge he was home in heaven before his body ever released him was comfort. Dave was a part of my life given-taken and now embracing it for what was. Peace and Comfort."

I did not know his daughter was on that website and the next morning there was a comment thanking me for my post. She wrote, "My Dad always spoke so fondly of you." I was sad reading this because I wondered how he went through life not contacting me or anyone else when I was alone for so long.

CHAPTER 7

Dave passed before the Christmas holidays of 2014. Instead of my mourning subsiding, it became a part of my daily life, so I returned to Healing Inspirations, the wonderful center that offered the metaphysical modalities I was so blessed to have found. I attended a message circle with Michele Love. A message circle is where a medium shares a message to each person from their guides and sometimes from loved ones who have passed on from the beyond. After the message circle, I asked Michele who taught the Twin Flames class if she understood why I was experiencing this deep grief. She said, "Meet your Twin Flame. Dave will be around you forever." I sincerely never connected this experience with her class on Twin Flame. I told her other practitioners were telling me to just throw this grief to the universe and move forward. They said, "You should let go of anything that doesn't serve you anymore." She laughed and said I could not discard or toss to the universe what I have as we have always been together as souls.

Everything Michele said was comforting, and I went home to check sources about Twin Souls on the internet. It was quite amazing to read the stories of people who met their Twin. Unfortunately for those who had a Twin that passed over, it described how the one left behind experienced physical, mental, and emotional pain. I resonated with these stories. The term *excruciating pain* was used—the exact words I would use to describe my life at that time. I do not want to be repetitive in my writing, but this desire to revisit my past and reconnect with Dave became a daily emotional roller coaster that brought no relief. These emotions would prompt me to contact mediums and others to reduce the pain and intense grief I felt.

A passage from "Grief Has No Closure," by Ashley Davis Bush LCSW, in *Psychology Today*:

> "We live in a culture that avoids emotional discomfort. In fact, our society makes it easy to look for distractions and diversions from all things painful. If we can drink, eat, shop, play, or Facebook grief away, we will.
>
> But here's the truth—losing a loved one is excruciatingly painful. And it doesn't just hurt for a few days, a few weeks, a few months, or even a few years. The impact of a major loss is lifelong. Emotional "closure" is a cultural myth.
>
> Why? Because no matter how many years go by—10, 20, 30—you will be changed irrevocably. You may think of your dear one almost daily and you will have days out of the blue that knock the wind right out of you. Certainly, the pain softens and eases over time. However, normal grief will always have moments of reoccurring sharpness, pain as raw as the very first day."

CHAPTER 8

The best daydreams of Dave are a waste. They cannot be lived out. When I see him in the dream, it's too hard to bear that he is so far away from my everyday life. Yes, it could be a delusion. It could be a message. It could be a test. Whatever this is, I can't stop putting myself under a microscope to understand why and what is happening to me. I quickly learned that blocking this grief would create more pain.

Without getting too detailed, in 2014 before his death, for the first time in 45 years, I had a strong urge to contact him. That year, I took up bowling after many years of not playing. I was pretty rusty, and I remember thinking if only I could call Dave and ask him to show me how to throw a curve. Dave was a bowler in the Professional Bowler Association. Who better to teach me how to follow through? So, I would throw the ball and, as I walked back, actually visualize him watching me throw the ball and it worked! I scored better when I did this. I chose not to search him out, as I believed he was in a relationship, and it just seemed selfish and inappropriate. I also never called him because the makeshift curve I tossed ended with me throwing my side out, leading to several chiropractor appointments and never bowling again.

During that year, I dated a guy for a few months—someone I should have dropped after the first date but didn't because I thought I was being too particular. I'd run into a friend, Steve, one of Dave's golf buddies at a local restaurant from time to time. I often wanted to ask Steve where they played so I could innocently show up. But the semi-commitment dating status I was in kept me from pursuing my curiosity. I often wondered if Steve told Dave he saw my dad and me. It may be my ego, but knowing Dave as I did, it would have been unlike him not to have said, "Tell Mon I said, 'Hi.'" After his death, I asked Steve if I ever came up in conversations and he said, "No". My gut said differently but I will never know. It did come up during a medium reading that Dave absolutely was sending a message and I never got it maybe even through another person. I always regret that my life was so complicated at the time that I did not ask Steve to send a message to Dave. This experience gave me such regret regardless of my questioning whether it would have been the ethical thing to do showing up at the course while dating.

CHAPTER 9

I soon learned that friends and family were not the people to seek out in this situation. I learned to hold it in until I could make an appointment to process my feelings with a counselor or a medium. Initially, I was so overwhelmed, I tried at times to find comfort talking with anyone who knew him. One person's response was, "Would you just let Dave die in peace?" The most painful response of those trying to help me was, "You need to get over it. Move on." Get over what? These comments were for them, not me. I would not intentionally put myself into this mental state, as I was not being fed anything about him physically or emotionally to encourage the thoughts. I had no idea how I could be in so much pain over someone I hadn't seen for decades. My life was busy enough, but this was new, and it would take time and money before I could find peace.

Why does this come back to haunt me? As I learned after months, the relationship he was in at the time of his death was not the healthiest for his easy-going personality. I also learned he was talking about leaving this relationship. Knowing this only increased my frustration. Why didn't I know this before? As in many stories of Twin Flames, this is exactly how it plays out. Lives of Twin Flames can run parallel where each knows there is absence of something, but they do not know what it actually is. I honestly would say to myself over the years and before his death that it seems someone is supposed to call me but isn't following through. I cannot express how many times this notion of someone not calling me went through my mind. Oddly enough, since his passing, I no longer ask myself that question.

One of the mediums shared that Dave is now aware of our soul connection and understands the reason for our separation. He doesn't want me to stay in this painful state but, instead, wants me to be brought back to my authentic self—as he knew me in our innocence and happiness. I am hoping to give back to him his very request as I work on myself daily.

CHAPTER 10

The emotional reaction I experienced each day did not make sense. I could not get him out of my head. I felt like I was a part of his family. I tried to be sensitive when contacting his family members, who were kind and seemed interested in what I was experiencing at first. Then, right about the same time, all three contacts—his sister, his niece, and his friend—would not return my calls. I asked for very little information and most definitely stayed away from asking for anything personal. They questioned why I did not contact him before this time, seeming to hint at blame. I tried to explain that to my knowledge Dave was in a relationship and I would not entertain intruding. Oddly enough, I had a medium come to my home and as soon as she walked into the room, knowing absolutely nothing of this, asked if "passive/aggressive" meant anything to me. I answered, "No." She asked again later. At the end of the session I shared my frustration of being shut out by family. She immediately said that was the passive/aggressiveness she sensed. Her background in psychology helped her understand how vulnerable I was, having shared my pain with the family, but then being left with their lack of empathy as to why I was experiencing such a heavy heart over Dave's death. For myself, if this was in reverse, I most definitely would want to know how a person experiencing such grief was doing from time to time. If he were alive, Dave would most definitely want to know how the person grieving was doing. That is just my personal belief.

CHAPTER 11

Years before Dave's death, I heard his mother was in the hospital, so I stopped by to visit her. It was wonderful anytime I saw her, but because of Dave's relationships I didn't always feel it was right to drop in as many times as she came to mind or as many times as I wanted to. It would be the last time I ever heard her say, "I wish you were my daughter-in-law." I asked if I could pray with her before I left, and we did. Within a day or two, I heard she had passed on. One of the psychics I met with later said her name and said she had been with me many lifetimes before. I wasn't sure whether to believe that but was amazed the psychic immediately said her name, Angie.

I saw Dave only two times in those 50 years since we dated. The first time was when visiting his newborn baby at his home, and the second at his mother's wake. I often thought about the wake, as he stood in line staring and smiling at me as I stood in the back. I can live that moment as if it was yesterday as it seemed he was trying to connect with me. I do not recall what I said to him in the receiving line, but I do remember his saying, "You're still beautiful." I didn't think too much about it meaning anything at the time.

CHAPTER 12

Before this event, my understanding of death was that it was final with no more communication or relationship with the departed. Dave's death though, brought a barrage of memories and thoughts of him so vivid, remembrance of good and bad times, sounds and funny expressions he made. People would ask, if this was the love of your life or your soul mate then why didn't the two of you stay together? I will need to go back to our initial meeting and dating experience to answer that.

The relationship began in my senior year of high school when I passed a classroom and heard a guy yell out, "Wait, who is she?!" It is so strange that I still remember the A-line green paisley dress my mother made that I was wearing. It was a good and modern look for the time. We later exchanged greetings and he asked me out. Dating Dave made going to high school fun and exciting. It was a very fast connection and romance, which really stepped up my interest in being in school every day. Our personalities were pretty opposite. I was a shy, naïve girl. He was an extrovert and had no problem fitting into any situation. Our opposite temperaments helped me feel better about myself while coming out of the awkward teen years.

My biggest challenge with him was his flirtatious personality, or at least that is how I viewed him back then. He was not threatening our relationship. I was not accustomed to so much high energy. I was more unsure of myself and, most likely, any long-term relationship or marriage would not have worked. I say this because many people back in the late 1960's were getting married after high school or college.

I do recall a lot of playful arguing and making up. Dave was so confident and cheerful, and, in my eyes, it always raised him above the bar the way he helped others. I looked up to him, but I was not grounded enough to see a lifetime together. He was the guy in the red convertible, who was always picking me up with the top down until I whined enough that he put it back up. I had that long, straight flipped hair with heavy bangs, like Marlo Thomas wore on the TV series *That Girl*, which was the style in those years. He had an infectious smile and always seemed free as a bird, laughing and living without a care in the world. When I think about it now, he truly lived in the moment and enjoyed life.

CHAPTER 13

To understand my love for Dave you need to know a little bit more about him. He was the son of a business owner in our small town. His mother absolutely adored me, and I really liked her. My mother very much accepted him and appreciated his respect for me. He had one brother and three sisters, and they were a pretty lively bunch. I recall our typical dates consisted of drive-in movies, bowling, dinners, Vernon Downs horse races, and car racing. He really knew how to treat a girl, and entertainment was always a part of the date. I found newspaper clippings of our friends' weddings. We actually stood up for three different weddings together. I have tried to retrace other significant events. If we had been allowed one more talk about our past, it would have given me so many more memories and answered so many more questions. I recall the dozen beautiful yellow roses, the large bottle of Shalimar perfume, and the most precious Valentine gift I ever received or even remember being given by anyone—a bowling ball with my initials. The beautiful yellow roses have come up in several medium readings.

I cannot remember how we parted. I know it was the era of the Vietnam War. He joined the Navy, as opposed to being drafted. I was flown down to Norfolk one weekend. On his weekend leaves, he would drive home to Syracuse from Virginia to see me. When I think back, he did it so effortlessly, but we were young and in love and so glad to be together. At some point, though, we parted ways. I believe it was me who ended the relationship. I found dating long distance extremely hard, and "out of sight, out of mind" was just easier. I believe in those early years we were both destined to paths that would keep us apart forever. It is so odd to me that the mental practice of shutting someone out of mind does not work now, especially after death.

CHAPTER 14

I found interest in my faith, but I became overzealous. I joined the Jesuit Volunteer Corps and was sent to the South Pacific and Oregon. My initial intention was good, but through the encouragement of very conservative Christians back home—not the Jesuits, instead of enjoying my life and my faith, I became very rigid and conservative. Books and tapes that were mailed to me, which I read diligently, had a further hardening effect on me. Little did I know this would take years to undo. The letter of those laws would be easier for me to live by than exercising my heart and trusting my God-given intuition.

When I returned home two years later, Dave was married. Oddly enough, I do remember thinking, *"He couldn't wait."* Now there was no reason for me to have thought this. We did not have a plan. It was just an odd thought that I will never forget having. A few years later, I married. My husband and I did visit Dave and his wife when they had their baby to bring a baby gift. I've asked myself why we did this and what prompted it? I think it was after a visit with his mother and learning of their child's birth that made me comfortable enough to contact them for a quick visit. Dave and my husband did know each other, so it wasn't too odd. Unfortunately, the one thing I will never forget was how quiet and subdued Dave was. That is sad for me to remember. For him, it was the beginning of a change that would eventually be a precursor to his future.

CHAPTER 15

I contacted a medium long distance. She said many things that convinced me that Dave and I still have a connection and that we were not mature enough when we were teenagers to have had a successful lasting relationship. She said it might be too early to really hear from him from the other side but advised me to practice meditation. Messages are received and given telepathically. Her reading saw me in a life lesson, but she told me not to spend all my time beating myself up for missing my opportunity while he was living. What I was experiencing was necessary. She encouraged me to remain open to what he brings. In response to this, three years later I can only say I truly try to live in the moment. There is a never-ending awareness though that something is missing, and that awareness brings Dave to the forefront. This grief has not stopped the momentum in my life, and I am doing everything I need to do. I could never use it as an excuse for not handling living day to day. I live to the fullest, aware of loss.

I also went to a counselor at a local bereavement center. The counselor was very interested in this story and sympathetic. She said, "This type of grieving would be harder to work through and may take longer than usual. It is not just his death, but also the missed experiences and opportunities over the many years you will grieve." She said she speaks to her husband, who she lost years before, every day. She advised me I would feel better if I tried. As a priest told me, "This person must have thought a great deal of you to have his presence in your life this strong. Be sure to talk to him often."

I know my emphasis throughout my story is on pain and confusion, but this is not like a headache or toothache where you understand where the pain is stemming from. The problem is the grief is so deep. It lets up for a while and then crashes down. I said the best prayers I have ever verbalized in my life. Michele Love once explained that grief is as if a part of your physical body has been removed. If all of a sudden you became an amputee, you would need to learn how to live without a leg or an arm. This analogy might be the closest way to explain things. It felt I was missing a piece of me. I had questions that I felt should be answered by now—especially, what do I do with this experience, and can someone just make this pain go away? This suffering intensified during hard times in my life, but I always knew there was a difference between the daily trials I was experiencing and his crossing over.

CHAPTER

16

I visited Coleen Shaugnessy, a psychic and angel reader. She said she would know instantly if this was Twin Flame or just a past love. She was very excited and said this was a Twin Flame and a connection for all time. She told me that this was not the first time we had been together. Her advice was that maybe this was too early for me to hear from him as other mediums had said. Meditating at that time was more painful then helpful. In time, meditation would be a time to look forward to. She asked me to trust my instincts, which most definitely would take more time.

A year later, another medium I met with saw three old Italian women dressed in black from head to toe, veil, and all. She and I did not understand what this meant. It was much later that I learned both Dave and my ancestors were from the same area of Italy. Our grandfathers were from northern Italy, or of Tyrol descent and from the same valley of Val de Chiese - Giudicarie. On our mothers' side, both families lived around Naples originally. I never knew his background, but this may be why I blurted out once to his sister, "I feel so close to you. I feel like we are family."

Another medium, Barbara Bennett, clairvoyantly saw Dave enter the room with me and stand behind me. Without knowing my concerns, she asked if my husband had passed. She surmised a strong commitment to spirituality that drew him to me. During the course of our session, Dave told her he felt responsible for missing opportunities to find me. She said this was a soul commitment we made but she was not sure how to fix it. This wouldn't be the last time I heard that we had many lifetimes together, but his life ended in a way no one would have anticipated. Dave's work on earth was done. My work was far from done. The medium's spiritual guides told her, though she had never heard of this type of encounter, that I was not faking my grief story. Through her, Dave said, "I don't want her to cry all the time for me." She added he will be watching me from afar sending love and prayers, an old soul looking after me. Barbara also said, "He wants you to enjoy the rest of your time here." He felt his male ego got in his way and to forgive him. I told her, "I did forgive him. I can't forgive myself right now." She said it's unusual for those who passed over to admit any fault, but that was not the last time I was to hear regret from him. I often am reminded that if I was not so invested in my spirituality, this experience may have gone unnoticed and been interpreted as something else that could have led me to a serious depression.

Barbara felt this was a situation where two souls promised to be together and weren't. Again this is typical of a Twin Flame. She looked at his picture and noted his "honest eyes." She told me he feels we missed a lot of moments because of him and missed the love and nurturing we both needed. He wishes he could fix the pain, but he will always be around. She encouraged me to talk to him and said he will answer in different ways. He is trying to apologize for not finding me and there is regret. The one thing she felt he strongly conveyed was his appreciation for my understanding him. As for me, I feel I understand him more now than I ever did in the past. Kidding, her last remark to him was, "You better be there when she crosses over."

CHAPTER

First letter to Dave:

How did I miss you? You were everywhere tonight in my mind. You were the 60s guy. I feel so sad knowing I have to ride this out with never a chance to run into you—never—so my imagination sees you as you were. It remembers our favorite pizza spot, splitting half a large pizza and our not having any problem devouring it, the looks you gave me and that wink, the infectious smile, the cool dresser you were. I miss you and haven't seen you in decades. It's not fair. I've wanted for so long to connect with someone that gets me. Pray for me as I do for you. Love, Mon

Second letter to Dave:

I wish we didn't meet in the 60s. I am forever searching to find a way to live with this. I made multiple mistakes, experienced much heartache, and then faced your passing. Ten months and it is still unclear how you came into my mind and heart so clearly. A day without remorse, grief and sadness would be nice, but not so. I can't go back. You can't come back. All chances gone—only questions left unanswered. Love, Mon

Third letter to Dave:

Not sure how to pray but sending you "love and prayers." I had so little money at that time to spend on practitioners to ease the pain emotionally and to see if there is a message from beyond was a necessity. You were not phony. You changed from everything I feared and became something I never would have wanted to happen to you. The women seemed domineering in your life and that changed the man I once knew. Your pain I inherited after you passed. I feel hopeless at times. I lived with anxiety from a loss that cannot be recovered. Desires that burn deeply as I cannot stop the desire to have you show up. There are places, music and memories that bring in such nostalgia that I am not blind to. I keep busy and involved to keep my sanity. Love, Mon

CHAPTER 18

Dear Dave,

I have few memories yet it's hard not to push a good memory away. Sometimes it's just being near your old family home that pulls me in. Regardless of the pain and sadness, remembering our few years is a comfort knowing I once had you and now, in a different realm, you are still around. Our lives seemed to be so busy over the past decades. From what little I learned, you were the one who served the relationship you were in and someone else was being waited on. You took little care of yourself, and your partner, who seems to have depended on you or co-depended on you, did not encourage your attending to your physical needs as one would expect in a relationship.

A year before your death a mutual friend of ours was discussing relationships with me. She never discussed you but at the wake felt it important to say, "I always thought the two of you would get back together." So it is odd that people knew our situations and no one said anything to encourage us to arrange a meeting. She was not the only one to state this and again another person who knew of my aloneness said nothing till you were gone. So it is odd people knew our conditions were far from happy and no one said anything to encourage us to arrange a meeting. I don't accept the saying "It's God's will," in this situation. I think this story holds substance because it is so unbelievable one would feel this much pain and truly feel such deep grief losing you. Love, Mon

CHAPTER

I don't know if I first saw it on Facebook or in my looking up information on the internet. I came across a retired private investigator, Bob Olsen, who researched death after the passing of his father. His podcast, called "Afterlife TV with Bob Olson" has famous people, doctors, and near-death experience survivors—just an incredibly interesting cast—telling their experiences. I tuned in because I was fascinated with learning something I had no knowledge of before. Learning of people who died and then returning to their body changed my understanding of life after death and took any fear out of dying.

As indicated before, with Twin Souls there is no such thing as closure. Twin souls always existed and will exist forever. There is nothing to close this experience. When I researched the experiences of Twin Flames or Souls, I learned from those who's partners have passed, the one left behind entered a very dark and "excruciating pain." That term was used over and over again from the testimonies I heard. I spoke with a woman who said she had this experience for 18 years after her marriage. I told her I do not have 18 years left. Oddly enough, one night flipping channels I saw a portion of the *Twilight* series. When Bella had thought she lost Edward, there was a scene where she woke at night screaming. I never woke at night screaming, but I did wake many nights keeled over in emotional pain and in grief that I could not stop the pain and the crying.

I am not sure, but this experience conveys a feeling my existence has been altered. There is an awareness more than I ever felt before that something is missing in my life. I can't deny what I am experiencing. When I am focused and doing a project, I am totally into it pushing and pushing myself all the time. It's not normal. This shouldn't be happening. I am caught in deep grief. I am a survivor and cannot play the victim role. When I am through with the project or work, the tears are released in relief. Some might think, *Maybe she is lonely and making up this fantasy.* Those thoughts could only be made by people who do not know me. There are millions of men out in the world, and as one of my best friends has said for years, "You could have anyone, but you will never just have anyone."

CHAPTER 20

I questioned Dave's choice of partners over those 45 years. What attracted them to each other? How? When? Was it ever life giving? When did the partnership stop being a partnership, or was she ever someone he fell in love with? What kept him from asking and accepting advice? These are questions I hoped the family would share with me. I think it would have been kind of them to help me process but respectfully I understood it could have been painful and kept them from moving on. It was easy to see they felt sorry for me and could not really understand an old partner's death having such a deep impact, when so little time had been spent together. Due to this lack of communication with his family, I realize I cannot convey in my story so much of what I don't remember or know about him. There had to be a spiritual connection that is not defined by our earthly walk as we know it. If nothing else, we most definitely were a part of a soul family from years past.

Several months later, a member of his family asked me had I been seeing Dave before his death. I emphatically said, "No. I wish I could say differently." I know they must have been talking and felt something had been going on between us before he died, but that is not so. I know it seemed impossible to believe that I could be experiencing grief, and it might have seemed that I was lying. I understand the family might not have delved into any possibilities on the spiritual level. Logically, it did not add up. I often prayed, "Why couldn't we have one meeting that would have eliminated this happening to me?" One meeting at least I could look back on and say, "No, we weren't interested, or yes, let's find a way." As I wrote earlier, at the time, I always was an "out of sight, out of mind" individual. Psychologically, this does not equate to who I became.

Being so torn and trying to accept this lack of closure was an everyday battle. I put myself down and I regretted that I ever spoke about it to anyone with outside metaphysical understanding. I operated my life fully and no one would ever know there was a war going on inside me. Regardless of being extremely selective about individuals with whom I would share, the person I confided in would just go silent. I felt people thought I was crazy. Denise McKee, a metaphysical friend and life coach, sympathized with my pain, but reminded me of something I experienced before this incident. Denise explained, "Look at what you went through over the past couple of years before he passed: adjusting to the loss of a job, a botched-up surgery, the role of caregiver, finances, etc. You are too hard on yourself. Dave also may have been so involved in his relationship and not questioning his future to have overlooked his heart concerns. His going to a doctor alone shows lack of self care at a critical time. Over the past years, I was looking at my problems, and the negativity I faced was overwhelming but not to the point I would not have had assistance going to a heart doctor during an episode of heart issues. I speak for him based on what I learned from his loved ones and the resonating messages from mediums.

Chapter 21

A note to self:

Nothing much has changed. The world is heavier. The world seems off, knowing he is not here. I have him floating in and out all the time in my mind. When I am alone it is the worst. No one can explain the tremendous flood of tears that flow—the words, the thoughts and the grief that grips me so deeply. I cannot help trying to resolve this and make the pain go away.

I frequented the gravesite at least twice a month and now living farther away go less seldom. It is where I want to go and talk regardless of all the talking and praying, I normally do. I know he is not there; but as I have read in articles on death, his spirit may have been a passenger in my car as I drove there. I change the arrangements in the vases according to the season and find this gratifying.

CHAPTER

With Twin Souls there is an undeniable and unconditional love regardless of their history, any hurt or broken promises. This unconditional understanding of another regardless of faults, sin and imperfection is key to me. I can honestly assert that nothing can be said to break my love and belief. My friend, Len, had a message from her mother after she passed. The message was, "Tell Len life goes on." She encouraged me that a Twin Flame is very real as the souls are one. She encouraged me to be gentle with myself and that he truly hears my words and is near.

Note included in a Christmas card to Dave's family:

> To Dave's wonderful family,
>
> His leaving has brought unexpected grief to me. I have spent the last 20 years alone feeling the only thing I can do is look back and be thankful I even had a relationship with Dave in my youth. We were very young, but he definitely left such an impression on me. I know when I was younger, I feared our differences and it scared me off. Now I

see his dedication, generosity and selflessness were something any woman would desire. I will not accept a relationship that shows no respect and respect is definitely what he gave me. For now, I spend time talking with him, visiting the cemetery, asking why I couldn't have run into him at least once when we could have taken a second look. As a friend put it, in those days, life was easier and carefree. We did not have the burdens we carry today. I was happy but after two divorces I have been so unhappy for far too long. I did not know his circumstances, but it would have been totally inappropriate to contact him anyway in his relationship.

Your family is so beautiful. Thank you for always being kind to me when it could have been so easy to ignore me. I know that angels were there when no one else was on that fateful day. Love, Monica

CHAPTER 23

A letter to Dave:

This has been another tearful week. I can't believe how I feel so much loss when you come to mind. I am not trying to punish myself with these thoughts. They are just made so real by the emotional pain I carry day after day. I am trying to force myself to listen to the music I am most moved by. They are the songs of our era. It always put me right with you then, and now it does the same. The difference is I can't stop crying when hearing it now, so I have refrained from listening to the music. I would say the best song (and there are many) that describes this is Kenny Rogers and Gladys Knight, "If We Knew Then What We Know Now." Back in the day, I would daydream and be anxious for your call or visit. I am asking you to send me someone in the interim. I am so unhappy. I listen to people who write their stories of true love, and people who find their partners from the past and start again. I did not have that with you. I didn't even get close to that, though I know you always wanted us to marry young. I love you Dave—I miss your smile, your funny ways, and just the physical companionship I need so much now. I'm writing this from a class in Memoir Writing. I question why anyone would want to read of someone's torment when I don't have enough answers why this is happening to me. The desires will be coming out more and more in my writing because they are ever there. Love, Mon

The past year, a local professional bowler friend of Dave, much older than he was, passed away. I read the obituary and felt anger and sadness that Dave died so young and went first. That day was extremely painful. I couldn't shake the heaviness and cried a lot. It felt like I fell in a hole. Plans to go out were cancelled. I never knew when to expect the highs and lows of grief. The next day was better, but I think the obituary triggered the anger of Dave passing too soon.

Later the next year I took on a temp job with the United States Bowling Congress, or the USBC, registering bowlers from around the world. It was a very powerful experience because it was like Dave was everywhere. I could see if he had never died, we surely would have met there. The work was fast and involved, so I was extremely focused. Driving home brought out all the emotions. Dave said to the last medium I spoke with that he believed the experience brought us full circle.

During these years I lived daily in pain trying to let go. This was a typical prayer delivered from a place of agony.

A letter to Archangel Azrael, the angel for those crossing over and those grieving:

I am of sound mind. I am in love. I am trying to understand how to survive. Where are you? So much has been put on me to survive and pull myself together. Where is the benefit and when does grieving become peaceful? I pray for Dave as he obviously had more to gain by leaving. Regardless I remember our interests and our playfulness. How does it resolve itself inside me? With all my communication to him, how can I be sure he cares what I feel or say? It's like this was the meanest trick anyone could ever play. I feel like the woman waiting on the shore for the sailor to come home but he never appears. Is this some joke? A meeting in a neutral place would have prevented all of this. But there was no meeting. No wonder his mother longed for our getting together. Who thought like this back then? It was like she was psychic.

CHAPTER 24

I've done so much work on myself, and from it I learned a life lesson that creates heart shock, pain, and loss from the past.

Lesson: We all experience voids in our life from time to time. This void in me is so real. I cannot find any experience—social interactions, food, or person—to fill the emptiness. I hate it. I do not live in the past, but reminders are comforting and at the same time can be incredibly painful. Understanding the spirit world is necessary, and it is unfortunate we are not better prepared to face loss when it happens. I have been a regular church-going person all my life but feel the teaching of death can be too ambiguous. I know there are certain spiritual passages, rites, resurrection, reincarnation, or whatever you subscribe to, but death and grief are not taught enough. My hope is that through this writing I will help someone who faces this experience to embrace the loss and be open.

I have my 1968 yearbook and have read his short comment at different times over the years and honestly could not bring up any feeling. After his death, I picked it up one day and read it as I had many times before. It had an impact on me that I was not anticipating. I completely fell apart and was afraid to read it again for another year.

It read:

> "Monica, To a wonderful and beautiful girl. You are the kind of girl I can't live without for too long. I will never forget the way we met and our first date. See you around and good luck in the future with "Dave." May God Bless You. Dave P.S. I Love You."

This certainly is not a love sonnet or poetry, but something about his feelings, his penmanship, an innocent space in time so many years ago now spoke to me clearly. I also found in my yearbook so many classmates who wished me well in the future with Dave. It is so odd to read this now.

CHAPTER 25

Since I have spent a good amount of time over the years working on myself, I question why I was given this experience when it could have been given to someone else who has never worked on themselves. Well, maybe because I would be just that type of person to delve into this and not let go until I have answers and can put this to rest by writing my story. A local author who inspired me with her journey over the loss of her husband is Anne Marie Higgins. In her book, *Dancing in Two Realms, A Love Story Beyond Death*, Ann Marie feels her spiritual bond with her husband has only become stronger since the time of his death. She quotes Ira Gershwin, "Deep unspeakable suffering may well be called a baptism, a regeneration, the initiation into a new state." I, too, resonate with this beautiful quote.

And I related to Anne Marie's experience. She writes, "Love after death is not expected. They tell you to move forward, don't wallow in the past; your loved one is gone. But they are wrong. Love after death is intensely deep and intimate. I was shocked by its hold on me. I never imagined our physical and emotional relationship could be deepened by our spiritual, soul connection in death."

For me this is true too. I have often said that regardless of not writing everything down, a story is being written in my head every day about Dave and me. She later writes of a friend who lost her husband during the Iraq war. They had only been together five years, "It is not the length of time spent with your loved one but the depth of love that matters most."

A few years earlier I had bought the book, *Enchanted One – The Portal to Love* by Sheila Applegate. I attended her workshop at Healing Inspirations, and I found her comments interesting and uplifting and purchased the book. The first read through, I knew I was not ready for it yet and would someday pick it up again. After Dave passed, I decided to retry reading her book, looking for comfort. In her book, she writes about her beloved husband getting killed in an accident where his car was struck by another car driven by drunk teens. I found that her level of spirituality had developed well beyond my own. She appeared accepting and forgiving of those who altered her life forever with their careless decision. She speaks of the three years it took her to work through her anger and depression. She then came to her portal of love to understand the deeper meaning of his death that would create more love and peace then she had ever known. Sheila writes:

> "But beyond that, it was the unfolding of a divine plan that would allow my beloved Twin Flame to serve the Creator in an even greater way than he could have on Earth. It would allow him to walk with me beyond any illusion of separation and expand his love and service to levels I could not even conceive of at the time. So how could I condemn the people or the choices that had created this circumstance? I could not."

Sometimes, when people lose someone to traumatic death it can create a deep desire to research the afterlife. I feel that some of our religious faiths dropped the ball by not teaching enough about death. It was always a mystery or area where myths and fear were created. This new understanding of life beyond my experience, of readings and of others' testimonies were beautiful, yet still I question why was I experiencing this? There isn't a day that passes I don't ask, "Why?"

CHAPTER
26

In a segment from *Oprah on Super Soul Sunday*, October 30, 2017, her guest, Dr. Brian Weiss discussed the many forms of angels from his book, *Miracles Happen*. Oprah says, "But the essence of that person, the heart, the love of that person, particularly if you've known them on earth, I find become more powerful because you are infused with that energy and that spirit in a way you never were before." Dr. Weiss replied, "Energy does not have boundaries."

I love this because he says that before we are reunited, they are with us. Over my lifetime, I was told of my sensitive nature, and I thought this was weakness. I now realize this sensitivity is my gift and has opened me to a whole new realm.

I have managed my life over these years always living in the now and able to do anything required, and it took over three years from the anniversary of his death to feel a little less burdened. Over the years I tried hypnotherapy, Emotional Freedom Technique, the Emotional Code, Reiki, mediumship, and many expensive means to stop the pain. As a person of strong faith, I saw metaphysical gifts as an extension of a solid faith I live. Prayer is the constant in my life, so that was my main lifeline, while waiting to receive peace and understanding. The holistic gifts helped pacify me after a most difficult shock to my system, giving me a gradual healing, but also bringing me closer to understanding Dave and why we are connected.

This past year, I took a few weeks off, escaping to another part of the world to renew and bring some closure before I return. I found peace and solace living in the moment volunteering on one of the Cook Islands in the South Pacific and embraced it. I held the memories, but never once was my loss of Dave forgotten or not held with appreciation and respect. As Dave said through a medium, this story is not over yet, and she has a close second she will meet.

I do believe Dave and I will see each other again. I do believe there was a deliberate connection to me that I was not asking to happen in this way. I do believe that I would never have spent over three years inspired to write this story for myself if it were not for his presence. The inspiration to share my story came from beyond and the years it took was the necessary time to bring in the answers I could digest, the healing and the decision to release this to publication.

It all started by looking at the pictures at the wake and wondering, how did I forget the essence of him? I will have answers for my experience that I believe will validate what I have already learned on this side. I pray for his soul. Every day, I pray for his family as if they were my own. I understand if this story is a turn off for those who never experienced anything like this or if it doesn't fit with others' beliefs. My Christian walk has always been an experience revealing to me how much I have yet to learn. Spirituality is a process lest our spiritual growth will stop. There is so much to learn in Earth's classroom.

Before submitting this for publishing, I went once more to a highly regarded and gifted local woman, Maura the Medium. She said Dave was aware of my writing and said he was my muse. He most definitely deserves the right to be labeled co-creator—divinely inspiring me through the writing. There were many affirmations in Maura's reading as to what I have believed and heard before of his presence. She was emphatic that this journey would not end but continue into the hereafter. He most definitely wanted me to stop writing and let it go as the gift it was intended to be in respect and honor of both of us. My releasing this story is just in time for his birthday. I felt that the story—of two people who have been misunderstood quite a bit and who lived not quite in a place that would have made life's journey easier to walk—needed to be told.

Maura said she saw him on a boat. I said that was funny because over the years I have collected pictures of boats that I visualized where my special someone and I would spend time. She felt that early on I had a higher intuitive ability that was drawing his presence in. Dave told her there was more significance to the pictures. We truly were two ships passing in the night. We did not intend to continue on this earthly plane, but this was far from over.

Since the decision to stop writing and publish the book, a huge weight was lifted off me. I sense sadness and grief but there is something significantly different. Regardless of my appearance on the outside, this release of my story brought a shift I could feel and has brought an inner peace that I have not had for over years. The release of this story is my gift to Dave and myself.

I am forever grateful for writers I have found who shared their experience, as they have helped me to strengthen my faith each day.

Regardless of how much I have described grief and sadness, I am aware these burdens are part of what I experienced but are not my identity, my life as a whole or my future. I hope and pray this book will bring hope and peace to anyone who has lost a loved one or is afraid of life beyond.

I was told years ago by Sr. Maureen D'Onofrio that my tears are a form of prayer, that tears express something far deeper than words. Tears help fertilize the soul … some call them holy tears. If so, Dave has been blessed with many prayers for his soul's journey. I would like to close with a very appropriate thought from Dr. Seuss, "Sometimes you will never know the value of a moment until it becomes a memory."

ACKNOWLEDGEMENTS

First, I have to acknowledge the women of Healing Inspirations. As I look back over the three years, each practitioner played a part in my journey. The practitioners are Betsy Sams, Michele Love, Deborah DeRusha, Sharon Quinn, Suzanne Masters, Krystal Martin Murphy, and Karen Scanlon, who also offered some editorial consultation.

I also acknowledge the beautiful members of a unique book club, Lorraine Paradise White and her encouraging mentoring practice, Cynde Forst, Kelly Murphy, Michele McLaughlin, and Suzanne Masters, who taught me the gift of tapping to release emotions.

Others who shared their experience, wisdom, and advice: Denise McKee, Doreena Clifton, Anne Marie Higgins, Sheila Applegate, Lenore Vaccarello, Sr. Maureen D'Onofrio, Lorraine Pagano, Maura the Medium, and Hope for the Bereaved.

I am grateful to my dear cousin, Barbara Davis, for her final copy edits. Finally, I extend my gratitude to the Oasis Writing Group. If it were not for them, I may have never started nor finished my story.

All of these people didn't just listen but understood the world of the spirit, and some encouraged my healing through writing. As I dealt with death and grief, I came to understand there is a greater inspiration from the beyond motivating this book. I would encourage writing in dealing with pain even if it is a few sentences, a word, anything to release emotions you do not want stuffed inside you but sent back to the Universe and to God.

EPILOGUE

Since I first wrote and had my memoir printed expressing my pain and deep grief, I have come to such a peaceful place. Today I heard him say that this experience is a reflection of us pure and perfect. I have no doubt that his death brought me to this place of understanding and acceptance of our physical body's rest. I am so thankful for this journey and for all the possibilities ahead.